THE PINK

W9-CLN-891

Kyle Schlesinger

The Pink, by Kyle Schlesinger
Chicago: Kenning Editions, 2008
www.kenningeditions.com

Cover design by Quemadura
www.quemadura.net

Order from Small Press Distribution
1341 Seventh Street, Berkeley CA 94710
www.spdbooks.org   1-800-869-7553

ISBN: 978-0-9767364-4-8

Grateful acknowledgement to the editors of the
journals in which some of these poems first
appeared: 5 *Trope*, *Damn the Caesars*, *Drill*, *London
Research Group for Artists' Publications*, *The Portable
Boog Reader*, and to the publishers of housepress
and Buffalo Vortex for producing two of these poems
as handbills.

THE PINK

MACROSEMANTIC LITURGY

There are plenty of rivers in the sea
But you can't step on the same fish twice

This page underwritten in part
By an unwritten point of departure

Teething on erasure
A botched Lacanian outline

In wobbly locomotion
A dull ache recedes

Levels the heart to starch
A cold foil rodeo thump

Reverses widely
And barley green

Once in an errant
Wake of kissing steers

Any addendum
Winters out

Ligatures alter
Curfew endure

Begrudged radiance
An inkling's last decision

Culled from curdling excess
Palisades entwine an oily outside

Molten ruin got the runs in
The spandex of forgetting

Images impale
An open digression

Swerves to smaller pages
Substantiate an aside

Dissolves end ellipsis as
Latency legumes conditionally

THE FUTURE CONTINUES ON THE NEXT PAGE

Centerline

Fold sheet
To obtain

Centerline

Center form
On bed

By means

Of line
On this

Bar folded sheet

Set side guide
The width of

The folded sheet

Away from
Centerline

On feed board

SHABBAT SALOON

The blue in the blueprint
Is the sensation of a concept

And the hue in the house
Is the concept of a sensation

No such thing
As a blue house

Any house of language
May appear opaque

On a transparent
Afternoon when

Linguists drop
Like duck phones

Tattoo blue
A grainy wonder

HEY NANCY

Meaning there will be a place to sit
Between the chair and thought of it

Have we arrived
And move

This time precludes
Light's lofty

Turn towards
The quotidian

But lichen a worm
In the beak to the

Bleak passage say
Take C to Kingston

Or the inversion
Susceptible to a tea

Take it that there is nothing
As pleasant as a pleasant day

Hereon herring white moss on a wire
The pond becomes a lark

Slinks to a crawl
At either intersection

SHEDDING
for Thom

Which consonant
Becomes in time
The overtone of a bird
Tear at this veil
To kiss or cry
To see red or white
White or red
As the opposing tones
Of departure

To parse
Which consonant
From which to
Which from
Moment to
Moment departure
Is becoming
Another islet's
Inroad out

Leapt for fresh
Water compound
Becomes in time
A view
From a room
A room parsed

Aside as you pause
Please read
Aeration for air

The air that comes
Up for air and
Again goes under
The overtone of a bird
Cut off center
Circles the literal
Equator of the
Mind's reasons'
Holding pattern

And if you think
This is too fast
Try rereading
One phrase
Tear at this veil
At a time when
Bedeviling coevals
Ease into luke
Warm water together

Again when all else
Pales by comparison
Composition is a form
Of literary allusion
A makeshift blackbox

To kiss or cry
Shifts meaning over
To you the reader then
Gives you the shaft

In the opening field
When a literary executor
Pampers a palimpsest I
Love talking dirty
In opposing tones
I write to be read
To see red or white
From your prospective
Ovation betwixt us

Sound waves crash
Over water an audio
Mirage over water
Passes through holes
Where holes get
Out of Os
On their own
White or red
Sunspots in holes

In the quicksand
Of sense lunacy shivers
Down the backdrop

The veil behind every
Collection of white
Heat waves recollection
Spinning out
Constantly
As the opposing tones

Of departure
As the opposing tones
White or red
To see red or white
To kiss or cry
Tear at this veil
The overtone of a bird
Becomes in time
Which consonant

LINER NOTES
for Ulf

Life comes in
The middle
So let's mingle a
Little while

At the tattoo parlor
We were faking out
Soviet tanks
You'll never get

A better balloon than
This so why not knot
The question that
Inhales you

It don't matter
What you had or didn't
It's what you did
When it wasn't

Look at the sea
Running like Kraftwerk
I'm my own Sisyphus
In syrupy flavors

Or better yet tsunami
There's not a shred
Of decency left
So call a spade

A spade on
Speakerphone
Because wedding soup
Like a pink pup

On brown never
Tasted better

OR SAY A MARK
for Alan

Turning calligraphic
Sea frozen over
The event falls
Through itself

These tides this
Time each time
It could have been
Mind's lagoon

Spools out ligatures
Lift backward
Over the handlebars
Verbatim

Thinking of
Things in their absence
Working with things
As they are to play

Back this quote
Culled from form
As if memory were the kind of
Chase one could set aside

Mull over some
Time or another
To say it here again
The leading of

A phrase could
Change a life

When a splinter in
The real writes the readers'

Writer out of
And above each body

A shoulder
And each shoulder a beard
And each beard a face
And each face faces another

As the serif in
The surf's curl
Pulls back the
Sand at your feet

SQUARELY

Squarely arch
Tracks heist
Dreaming figures
Nude new zeal
Socialism drains

A more pliable
Tomorrow again
Suecessions step
Carnations for
Plausible thaws

Forgetting disclosure
Stepping through
One tires of
Another
Someone else

Always here we do
Not know the water
With water

CARNATION

We hoist as we hoist
Consider storms wallop
Viola windows glare pines sap
Glades delight stumble through
Rubble and stubble

Along the strings lead
Pipes drain blister
A perfect fourth
Birth defects
Sand piper corridor

Iridescent tolls
Just a jeep road heaps
Launder in luxury construction cites
Blight in cursive
Salutations fascinate landmines

Parachutes fall from
Sky goes white dilate
Sun sums up
The afternoon spent
Fog air error

TREATISE

But beauty resembles what it
Cannot absorb the gill wilt

Faint light maneuvers
One sense or another

Coriander like a good soup ladles lentils
Love a cold war

Some hooligan's sneakers sucker
Punch the sidecar

Oasis doesn't detract from formal
Frontal intention

Along an excavation
A ballistic curve

No sleet shines like the present
The shivering shoe passes

Look before you leap but keep the creep
Out of my lap

The only access road I know is abscessed
Malignant encounters of the third kind

Dorantes, Dolores. *sexoPUROsexoVELOZ and Septiembre: A Bilingual Edition of Books Two and Three of Dolores Dorantes, by Dolores Dorantes*. Jen Hofer trans. Published with Counterpath Press. ISBN 978-0-9767364-2-4 $14.95

Guest, Barbara and Kevin Killian. *Often: A Play*. [out of print]

Larsen, David. *Syrup Hits*. [out of print]

Lu, Pamela. *Ambient Parking Lot*. [forthcoming]

Mohammad, K. Silem. *Hovercraft*. $6.00

Scalapino, Leslie and others. *Kenning 12/WAY* audio CD. ISSN 1526-3428 $15.00

Schlesinger, Kyle. *The Pink*. ISBN 978-0-9767364-4-8 $7.50

Seldess, Jesse. *Who Opens*. ISBN 0-9767364-0-3 $12.95

Thomas, Lorenzo. *Time Step*. [out of print]

Weiner, Hannah. *Country Girl*. [out of print]

Weiner, Hannah. *Hannah Weiner's Open House*. Patrick Durgin ed. ISBN 0-9767364-1-1 $14.95

www.kenningeditions.com

www.spdbooks.org